W9-BGC-369

Hammer

hammer POEMS
Mark Turpin

Sarabande Books
LOUISVILLE, KENTUCKY

No part of this book may be reproduced without written permission of the publisher. Please direct inquiries to:

Managing Editor
Sarabande Books, Inc.
2234 Dundee Road, Suite 200
Louisville, KY 40205

Library of Congress Cataloging-in-Publication Data

Turpin, Mark.
    Hammer : poems / by Mark Turpin.— 1st ed.
        p.   cm.
    ISBN 1-889330-85-X (hardcover : alk. paper) — ISBN 1-889330-86-8
(pbk. : alk. paper)
I. Title.
PS3620.U77 H36 2003
811'.6—dc21   2002012986

Cover and text design by Charles Casey Martin

Manufactured in the United States of America
This book is printed on acid-free paper.

Sarabande Books is a nonprofit literary organization.

 This project is supported in part
by an award from the
National Endowment for the Arts.

FIRST EDITION

For Dumah K. Frazier
who gave me a trade

Contents

Acknowledgments   9

ONE A Carpenter's Body   11

Laborer's Code   13
The Box   14
Last Hired   15
Pickwork   17
Shithouse   19
Poem   20
Hammer   21
Sonnet   23
Don Fargo & Sons   24
The Man Who Built This House   26
Carpenter   29
Waiting for Lumber   31
A Carpenter's Body   33

TWO   35

Millet's *Shepherdess with her Flock*   37
Photograph From Antietam   39

THREE   41

Will Turpin b. 1987   43
In Winter   44
Aubade   46
The Furrow   47
The Day   48

FOUR   49

Sledgehammer's Song   51
Finish Work (after Hardy)   53
Gene Lance   54
Before Groundbreak   55

FIVE   The World of Things   57

Setting Up   59
The World of Things   60
Jobsite Wind   61
Nailer   63
Downslope   66
Foundation   68
The Aftermath   69
Everything Under The Sun   71
Muse,   74

The Author   77

Acknowledgments

Grateful acknowledgment is made to the editors of the following publications in which these poems first appeared, sometimes in slightly different form:

Agni: "Everything Under the Sun," "Downslope"
Berkeley Poetry Review: "Nailer"
The Boston Phoenix: "Quiet Son"
Boston Review: "The Box," "Pickwork," "Shithouse," "In Winter,"
                    "Will Turpin b. 1987," "Photograph from Antietam"
The Paris Review: "Pickwork," "The Box"
Ploughshares: "Photograph from Antietam," "Before Groundbreak"
Poetry Flash: "Nailer"
Red Rock Review: "Millet's *Shepherdess with her Flock*"
Slate: "Jobsite Wind" "Waiting for Lumber"
The Threepenny Review: "A Carpenter's Body," "Laborer's Code,"
                    "Sledgehammer's Song"
Tarpaulin Sky: "The Furrow," "The Day"

The Handbook of Heartbreak, edited by Robert Pinsky: "Last Hired"
Take Three: Two, Agni New Poets Series: "Nailer"

A Carpenter's Body

Laborer's Code

A plot plan tells a history of a lot before a job,
the surveyor's name and number, year he drove his stakes
and set sea-level elevations of hubs and monuments

—but the laborer has never seen it. He doesn't give a shit,
piecemeal is his stock-in-trade: to this depth
the ground is razed and that—the string stretched there—

is the property line, sagging across the view.
Sunlight bears on the stack of studs where lunch hour goes
in an arc of exhausted silence. He rips a bag of chips,

pops a coke. The front page is news; he talks
fishing trip, violence, checks, half-aware he's said
it all before—what more can he say?

When it's time, he stands and throws
mere fill in shovelwidths somewhere over his left shoulder
for the pleasure of shoving the shovel in.

The Box

When I see driven nails I think of the hammer and the hand,
his mood, the weather, the time of year, what he packed
for lunch, how built up was the house,
the neighborhood, could he see another job from here?

And where was the lumber stacked, in what closet
stood the nail kegs, where did the boss unroll
the plans, which room was chosen for lunch? And where
did the sun strike first? Which wall cut the wind?

What was the picture in his mind as the hammer
hit the nail? A conversation? Another joke, a cigarette
or Friday, getting drunk, a woman, his wife, his youngest
kid or a side job he planned to make ends meet?

Maybe he pictured just the nail,
the slight swirl in the center of the head and raised
the hammer, and brought it down with fury and with skill
and sank it with a single blow.

Not a difficult trick for a journeyman, no harder
than figuring stairs or a hip-and-valley roof
or staking out a lot, but neither is a house,
a house is just a box fastened with thousands of nails.

Last Hired

On Monday returned the man I fired
wanting the phone number of the laborer he loaned money to,
and stood while I wrote it out on a scrap of shingle
and the crew on the floor kept hammering

with the silence of three hammers tapping out different beats.
I scratched down the name and seven digits with a flat pencil,
scrawling across the ridged grain and then with it.
He thanked me with an uncomfortable smile and left.

He was incompetent, but incompetence is not a crime
—I never liked him.
Out of almost pure intuition, right from the beginning
and I noticed how quickly the other men closed in beside me

against him. He must have felt it, too,
those days as he knocked the nails out of his screwed-up formwork,
and spit saliva in the hammermarks of his windowsills
to raise the grain. Must have every day

felt more alone. He had a habit of mumbling explanations
that trailed into incoherence. But he was not a stupid man.
When I asked him to repeat himself, he shrugged me off
with a sigh and asked me what I wanted him to do.

The morning I fired him I walked down to the street
before he could leave his truck, and was on the way surprised
and annoyed by a hypocritical watering in my eyes that went away.
Then catching him, saw-in-hand, I told him to go back to the truck.

I said it deliberately hard, so he would guess
before I said the words. Then we stood together. And he took it
as if he expected, and failure were something he had grown around.
Then he got in his truck, drove the street, and was gone.

Pickwork

There is skill to it, how you hold your back all day, the dole
of force behind the stroke, the size of bite, where
to hit, and knowing behind each swing a thousand others wait
in an eight-hour day.

And if the head suddenly comes rattling down the handle:
knowing to drive a nail for a wedge between the wood and the steel.
The inexperienced pretend to see in the dirt a face they hate,
and exhaust themselves. The best

measure themselves against an arbitrary goal, this much
before lunch, before break, before a drink of water, and then
do it. Some listen to the pleasant ringing
of the pick, or music, and trancelike, follow the rhythm

of the swing. Once I spent a half hour attentive
only to my muscles triggering into motion, sweat
creeping down my chest. Ground makes the biggest difference.
In sandstone you feel the impact to your knees,

in mud you yank the point from the muck each throw.
The hardest part is not to let the rhythm fail,
like stopping too often to remeasure the depth, stalling
in the shithouse, losing self-respect, or beginning to doubt:

Am I cutting too wide? Is the line still straight?
Or thinking of backhoes, more help, quibbling inches
with the boss. On my job Lorenzo works in the sun all day,
his silver radio quietly tuned to the Mexican station.

Shoveling out, he shrugs and says, "No problem, Mark,"
waist-deep in the hole.
From the spot I work, I hear the strike of his pick all day.
Driving home together he has told me about his two black whores,

his ex and daughter in LA, and Susan Nero, "on-stage." Thirteen
    times
he's seen her. Almost reverent, he says, "She is so beautiful,"
and makes immense cups with his hands.
And driving home he has told me of his landlord who extorts him

for the green card he doesn't have, of his "mo-ther"
dying of cancer in Mexico City, of his son-of-a-bitch
dad who beat him, and her, and ran away, of his brother Michael,
and Joaquim, in Chicago, the central valley. In the car

he asks me if I think the boss will hold half his pay, he needs
to save something for his sister
—I hear his pick all day
and in the afternoon I go out to ask him, how's it going?

He shrugs me off. "It's no big problem, Mark.
No problem, I can do it, but the fucking pick is dull,"
and shows me the blunted steel point. "I need something—
sharper, you know: I need a sharper pick."

Shithouse

Illiterate, banal, scrawled in ink, fingered in shit,
even blood—or penciled painstakingly
until lead clung to the letters ploughed

into the plastic wall;
some messages so impersonal they surprise by the need
to be said at all: Fuck.

Others are illumined with autonomous cocks and balls,
spread female legs like wings
with the cunt scratched furiously.

One I saw, a squirrel, his face void of expression
except intentness, licking
his own huge human-sized dick and balls—as if cracking a nut,

the four black marking-penned
spurts of cum, in parody of tears, falling from it;
the figure obviously worked on

to get it right:
forearms like crazed wires where he labored
frustrated to fix how they cross the torso,

the tiny strokes of scrotum hairs
coaxed from the blunt black pen, the gratuitous branch—
as if loathing were art. As if it weren't.

Poem

What weakness of mind gripped a moment's meanness tighter
than his?—stalling, reeling, retarding at the thought that
cupped the vision of the rope actually smoking through his hands
—while elsewhere and peripheral, a huge tree-limb plummeted.
The rope, as he observed it, was not a thing, not an object,
but a slender field of havoc twisted to a strand which, though he
opened the grasp of his hands from pain of it, would not leave
    his hands
(unless he thinks of something yet to do.) But he did not—
not immediately, and later he would raise his hands, and marvel,
grin, almost feel a joy at recognition of that groove
the rope burned and furrowed across the flesh of each;
he could plainly see its path in blood, blisters, and burnished skin
from finger to finger as if it were something caught that was
rarely caught. He held his hands up as evidence of something.

Hammer

Head-heavy, hickory worn
to a walnut color,
you get to know its feel,
how the ripping-claw curves
and tapers to a chisel edge,
the rising tone of the nail
till it sinks and the hammer thuds.

Or pulling it up suddenly
off a nailhead like a button—
letting it ring in the air.
Gene Lance showed me how
to never miss and kept fingers
pinched around the nail
as he drove it in.

Hands and fingers: ten-odd
cuts, blisters, splinters,
none bad enough to pull,
the smooth crescent bulge
of a fingernail growing back in,
a framing callus. Missing once
I blackened my eye knocking

off a brace, and once took
a splinter the size of a pencil
beneath the vein in my right arm.
The carpenter Chris fired,
he felt the hammer his last day,

raising a big wall that broke free
and collapsed, all of us getting

away but him, left crumpled
and pinned beneath the studs,
the wall bearing on his collarbone,
his cocaine habit, divorce, $50,000 debt
to the rehabilitation clinic (Chris
said he was just tired of hearing him
say cunt all day)—dragged

convulsive across the floor, the builder's
wife posed beside his head, sunlight
harsh across the plywood floor
except for the shade his body made—
and Chris, guilty, blind, hectoring,
hammer-in-hand, lining the men up
to raise the wall again.

Sonnet

Too much for them, too cold and unready
for much, but to stand, shiver and blow
cold breath on cold hands, sheltered in the bowels
of a house. Brick grade beam, mudsill, old dust,
divots of waste. They talk to cut the chill,
each wishing he were somewhere else
though no one ponders how he got here.
Each knows what truck, what drug, what wife
and tells the story to himself each half hour
as hammers fall and fall, as desire freezes
his nose. In work-lamp light they stamp or wander
into the dim, shiver in their clothes and smoke.
The others there, but not there, really,
not like a cold like fire on his skin.

Don Fargo & Sons

Helpless to throw them away
or to use them unaltered,
for years he crossed out *& Sons*
on the tiny invoice pads

from a cardboard box too tall
to fit beneath the seat.
His blackened mechanic's hands
turning the slip of carbon.

At seventy, he needed help up
the site's steep slope to the hoe.
Two laborers and him up
the loose hillside, or him by himself,

hauled by a cable from the loader's winch,
grasped with grim embarrassment.
Then, arriving, he spat and pissed
onto the bucket of the hoe

before he climbed to the seat,
as all smiled. Tall, craggy, with
a big-voiced drawl, he learned
to operate a backhoe in Korea.

There was no gentleness, only
precision in the swing of the hoe
with Don in the seat as the arm
swung from pit to pile in flowing,

boxlike movement, dripping grease.
I recall the blandness of his look in the sun
as the bucket tore the ground we
stood on and the backhoe rocked.

I never asked if he loved his work,
or if a day's glorious vulgarity
was why he still got up at seventy.
His gift was not seeming to try.

The Man Who Built This House

First realize he didn't build it for himself,
and that changes a man, and the way he thinks
about building a house. There is joy but
it's a colder type—he'd as easily joy in
tearing it down, as we have done, down
to the bare frame, loaded boxes of lath
and plaster, stirring a dust unstirred since
well, we know the date: Thursday, June 19, 1930.
Date on the newspaper stuffed between
the doorbell battery and the box it lodged in.
Not so long ago, seventy years, historical
only to a Californian. The headline: "Admiral Byrd
Given Welcome In N.Y." "Rear Admiral
Richard E. Byrd, conqueror of the South Pole."
Safe to say, the man who built this house
is gone or nearly gone by now—and we think
of the houses we have built, and the strangers
who will certainly, eventually come to change
or tear them down—that further event that
needs to happen. And there is a foulness
to this dust, dust locked in walls till
we arrived to release it to the world again.
So, maybe, all is as it should be. Still, the man
himself haunts me. I noticed it—especially
after my apprentice saw fit to criticize his work,
this neat but spindly frame of rough 2x4's—
2x4's for the walls, the rafters, even for the ceiling joists
(that he tied to the ridge to keep the ceiling from sagging)
that functioned adequately all these years

till we knocked it loose. And so, for reasons
my apprentice wouldn't understand, I admit
a liking, yes, for him and for this sketch
of a house, the lightness of his eye, as if
there might be something else to think about:
a sister taken sick, or maybe just a book or
a newspaper with a coffee and a smoke, as if
to say to the world: *This is all you take from me.*
Of course, having lived here a month already,
I know better—accustomed now to the
hieroglyphs of his keel marks, his red crayon
with an arrow denoting the sole plate of a wall,
imaginary, invisible lines that he
unknowing, passes on to me, numbers and lines
radiating from the corners and the eaves
—where the bird nests hide inside the vents—
all lining up, falling plumb, coming square and true
for me, and all his offhand easiness just a guise
for a mind too quick ever to be satisfied
—just moving quickly through the motions.
And, now, what he has to show for it, hauled away
in boxes and bags, and me about to alter
what's left—not like Byrd's Pole, fixed
forever. The pure radiating lines forever
flowing and unalterable—lines of mind only,
without a house attached. And yet, even a South Pole
doesn't seem much of an accomplishment to us—
to have merely found another place on Earth.
There is a special pity that we reserve
for the dead, trapped in their newspapers'
images of time, wearing what they wore,
doing what they did. I feel as much for this man here,
and for the force it took to pull a chalked string

off the floor, let it snap, and, make a wall.
Something apart from something else,
not forever but for a little while.
He must have felt it too, a man like him,
else why leave the newspaper for us?

Carpenter

Unasked, he once said what he required of life
and I was more surprised by the occasion of his
telling me than by his simple words:
rest when he got home, beer, and sports on tv;

he said it earnestly without swagger or resignation,
with the pride and appraisal of a man who perceived
himself ordinary and wanted what he had.
And I wondered if his flatness was meant to be

a check to me, carpenter, same as him but with desires
flagrant and helplessly exposed by the years.
He held the rope while I drove nails
at the edge of a steep roof above a sixty-foot drop.

I trusted him not because he was the least imaginative
but because he understood and accepted that I was scared.
A kind of respect really. As much as I longed
to tell my secrets he kept his mostly,

sitting on the ridge awkwardly transferring
a cigarette from hand to lip
as he adjusted the rope around his back and down to me—
occasionally holding it with one hand

as he took a drag, though not thoughtlessly.
He tied steel his first day, an apprentice
from the union accustomed to abuse, his hands clumsy
with the linesman's pliers but fast

from effort instead of skill—the sharp wire
leaving a dozen marks of his work
on the back of his hands before lunch.
In the union he only learned to run shearwall,

miles of it, but these mornings walking with cigarette
and coffee from his truck he asks about the day:
"What's up?" regarding me on his heels,
having learned most of what I've taught.

Now with a family at thirty-four his belly sags,
and when he runs the bases he comes back to the bench
with pain in his chest. On the phone his wife tells me
of him standing in her kitchen, tool belt on,

with the six-foot level I gave him for his birthday,
saying "Hey Hon, look!" And on the jobsite
we crown and cut a beam that we will raise to span
two gables and support the rafters on the roof

while discussing how to set the ladders, and who gets which
end: getting tasks and calls straight—then leaning, reaching
from his ladder, guiding the beam to the wall he grins
at me grimacing, anticipates the weight.

Waiting for Lumber

Somehow none of us knew exactly
what time it was supposed to come.
So there we were, all of us, five men
at how much an hour given to picking
at blades of grass, tossing pebbles
at the curb, with nothing in the space
between the two red cones, and no distant
downshift of a roaring truck grinding
steadily toward us uphill. Someone thought
maybe one of us should go back to town
to call, but no one did, and no one gave
the order to. It was as if each to himself
had called a kind of strike, brought a halt,
locked out any impulse back to work.
What was work in our lives anyway?
No one recalled a moment of saying yes
to hammer and saw, or anything else.
Each looked to the others for some defining
move—the way at lunch without a word
all would start to rise when the foreman
closed the lid of his lunchbox—but
none came. The senior of us leaned
against a peach tree marked for demolition,
seemed almost careful not to give a sign.
And I, as I am likely to do—and who
knows, but maybe we all were—beginning
to notice the others there, and ourselves
among them, as if we could be strangers suddenly,
like those few evenings we had chosen to meet

at some bar and appeared to each other
in our street clothes—that was the sense—
of a glass over a fellow creature's fate.
A hundred feet above our stillness
on the ground we could hear a breeze
that seemed to blow the moment past,
trifling with the leaves; we watched
a ranging hawk float past. It was the time
of morning when housewives return
alone from morning errands. Something
we had all witnessed a hundred times before,
but this time with new interest. And all of us
felt the slight loosening of the way things were,
as if working or not working were a matter
of choice, and who we were didn't
matter, if not always, at least for that hour.

A Carpenter's Body

I'd seen them near the end of their days
straightening against the springs of a pickup seat,
pulling the door closed. Signaling us
with a wave, everything would be okay.

Quickness that once shouldered a beam,
that cool leverage of strength and skill
scissors to a final apex, and then, one simply feels
one's hands opening, the weight serious.

Dee on his knees troweling cement.
Gene's glowing fridge of vodka and steak.
Christopher's laments: dear god
one needs to be an expert now.

The best resort for incompetency
is comment on failure, a large collection
of tools. I could quit. I have driven my share.
There are other ways to toil—to build a house is

a fine trade in youth; in age it must be
a religion. Rain spreading on the sodden site.
Stacked lumber steaming in sun's beams, that
rough geometry risen by a joy in brawn.

two

Millet's *Shepherdess with her Flock*

I know you, girl, like one of mine, how
you know each of them: particular
but not personal—"the stupid one, lame
in the left forefoot" or "the one who hates
the gate." Your back turned to everything.
And why shouldn't it be? You know all
the shades of fleece. Like the color of
the sky your back is turned to, as if it were
the only sky. Millet meant it to be—
how the sun is promising something
it probably won't deliver behind clouds
that may never break but stretch into
afternoon, telling you: life is this hallowed
pause. Maybe. You aren't leaning on
your staff. Rather, it leans on you.
It is only your time living asks you for.
I thought at first you might be knitting,
but no, thank god, you're not. You are
what? Studying your thumbs absently—
it's okay, your twelve-year-old mind
equaling the horizon, according to Millet.
And the dog in silhouette illustrates
the difference between human and beast:
he is paying attention to the sheep. He is
good at his job, focused if disappointed,
expecting something to happen that you
know will not. And the sheep press
back to back, never content without
that presence there. So unlike the wooly

dandelions that press up at your feet,
one here and there only, yet each one too
being nothing without the sun lighting its
lamp of seed. I suppose you could be
tearing a dandelion between your thumbs.
Millet says it's not for us to know.
The ground at your feet, though, is
important, and proof, in clumps of earth,
and yellow and brown twists of grass
and weeds, that everything is important,
and your aloofness, whether petulance
or patience, proof of human grace.
The clunky boots, your straight back,
your pink cheeks, the cold, the bulk
of woolen clothing that obscures your
girlhood, and weighs upon you exactly,
reminding you of the earth, reminds me
that to labor is a spiritual condition.

Photograph From Antietam

Around him is battlefield litter,
dew-swollen lumps of a spilled powder. What is it?
And the strips of cloth. Left behind
the lines of men that advanced or fell farther on

or hid somehow on this trampled field
of Maryland grass. By chance, at the extreme upper
edge of the photo—"unmistakable, but barely discernible
in the distance"—soldiers dragged into a long row,

their uniforms, the dark Union "Shoddy" or Confederate gray,
and the white? White hairy stomach and thigh of a Union man
whose trousers were left undone
by soldiers who looked at the wound and crawled off?

—Hardly more than unfocused grayscale. But here on the ground
photographed is one dead: sharp as a flower
and sprawled in the posture of ease,
one bent arm behind his head.

From the waist down it is hard to tell
his legs from bedding, his form is lost in rags,
his chest protrudes contortedly from a nest of rags.
Both sleeves are rolled, and a vein

in the crooked forearm still seems to bulge—
the other lies on his chest, pale and marble, feminine,
hand hidden at the wrist.
From the nose and eye, two dried black tears

of blood streak his cheek and forehead.
On his chin: two tufts of a cleft goatee, a devil's beard
—maybe he was a devil—he seems so young,
tossed and wrecked by the war.

In the zone of sharpness and contrast around his form
the blades of grass and sticks
seem to turn around him, the configuration of each twig
and clump of moss

quite apparent, yet abstracted into a circle
of random and spiked white signs
floating around him in nature's meaningless codes
for mishap or premature death.

You can see he lies in the shallowest of crevices,
not man-dug—as if pubes of the earth were
already forming up and around, drawing him back in—
a pitiful breastworks.

Likely it was only a spot where he had chosen to fire temporarily,
crossing this field. Or a friend pulled him here dying,
or he came to it himself during the battle
to prevent being wounded again.

three

Will Turpin b. 1987

The eyes are slits—the pupils grayest blue.
The eyebrows: two watercolor lines,
brush dipped only in water. On the nose's tip

is a minute field of white pimples....
Sucking so far is what he does best,
pulling with short intent strokes, or recklessly

(for the pleasure of recklessness it seems)
releasing the rubber nipple almost to the tip
then sucking in hard.

When it drops out he cries, feels the brush
of lips across his face, cooing; then pacified,
sucks again, follows motion with his eyes.

In Winter

These days in winter when the weather breaks for a spell
I return to the job thinking about
children, money, and divorce—

and sweep sliding pools of sawdust and rainwater
off the bloated plywood floor.
The rooms: dripping, dark—

smell of cigarette smoke, fir, and wool
as men splash from room to room in rubber boots and slickers,
nailing up the power cords from the water.

I'm amazed I'm here sometimes, doing this work with these men,
and sometimes expect them to find me out—though they never act
as if I am not where I am supposed to be.

They smile and joke with me, respect me.
Outside the frame of a window I see stumps of three plum trees
that yesterday we cut down with a chain saw—

and where the branches fell into puddles among the hillocks
of mud the water is stained a wine red—
and a shower of pale pink petals rings the dumpster.

When I lived with her, I never thought about my daughter
during the day, while I worked, while she sat in school
among strangers' children. Or if I did

it was with a kind of mustered poignance—
she would be there when I got home. But now, thinking of her,
I remember sitting in wooden chairs,

boredom, anxiety, and guilt swirling in my head,
what I was required to know but didn't
about Asia, mathematics, what someone said.

Aubade

Because of the enormous trees standing just outside,
dawn won't reach their bedroom windows for hours,
though already a jay cackles and flashes past,

each mullioned pane framing a blur of blue.
Strangely awake, he watches this, and talks
to her, though she is asleep, wants and needs

to sleep, but answers him sweetly with a little girl's
voice that seemed to him so uncharacteristic when
they were first together. Sitting up, he is naked

under the covers. And asleep next to him, she is naked
under the covers. Though not exactly amorous, he hooks
his knee over her hip, and pets her, and she arches

under his hand. And though not feeling particularly
loving and in fact, thinking of it as a little cruel,
he whispers he loves her into her ear, enjoying

her pleasure at it. He does love her.
And he strokes her again, though this touch undoes
the others, tells her to go to sleep.

Also cruel, he thinks, still strangely awake, and watches
the feeding jay turn, pump his winged shoulders twice
and disappear into the oak tree.

The Furrow

Your father must have held you up beneath the arms
to see your grandfather's body. What you saw
you don't remember, just a memory of yourself
seeing and the feeling of hanging in his hands.
Maybe he believed the only answer was to see,
and raised you up as if to say: Look—nothing
is there. Sadness then was only a lesson to recite
in the heart, wanting earnestly to please, attentive
to the soberness that buttoned a white dress shirt,
snugged a dark tie against your Adam's apple.

Rushing homeward in the dim back seat—anywhere
you might have stopped on the road that night:
those familiar furrows of dust when you got out
to pee in the gloom of the Central Valley, your
figure hidden in the shade of vines while the stars
above the highway churned. Half of everyone you
would ever love waiting back in the car as the engine
cooled, their voices eased beneath the whirr of crickets.
Forty years past. What lessons learned? Few, or none—
mainly the force of life behind now, raising you up.

The Day

Again you found yourself hoping for the last day,
to be like a man whose debts are paid and rises
with the sun to walk to work alone through a green valley.

The birds he cannot name, the sun shines as he remembered
it did. His shoes kick up tiny clouds of dust on the path.
He hums idly and carries his coat under his arm.

He thinks of a lewd joke to tell his wife in the kitchen,
vows to spend more time with his children. How wonderful,
he thinks it is, to be a righteous man.

four

Sledgehammer's Song

The way you hold the haft,
The way it climbs a curve,
   A manswung curve,
The way it undoes what was done.
The way a stake sinks,
   Cement splits or a stud
   Spins off its nails.

The way shoulders shrug.
The way the breezes waft
   And wake and tease a cheek,
The way it undoes what was done.
The way a cabinet cracks
   And rakes and bares
   The nail-scarred wall beneath.

The way a stance is spread,
The way the steel head pings
   And thrums and thuds,
The way it undoes what was done.
The way a bathtub breaks:
   Pieces barrowed, porcelain
   Left in a bin.

The way sight is stark.
The way the weight wills the arms,
   The back and heart,
The way it undoes what was done.

The way the weight is weighed,
   Stalling the swing,
   The sorrow mid-arc.

Finish Work (after Hardy)

> *Look back and see how past eternities of time*
> *Are nothing to us.*
>
> —Lucretius

Certainly he's dead now.
How long has it been
Since I thought of him?

What memory adheres?
There was a door he
Hung one afternoon

In a public building,
An office of the city,
Bookkeepers of a sort—

A pretty receptionist—
Oh, how he hung that door!
Not a gap of light

When he laid his six
Foot level up upon
The true of the jamb!

No doubt it hangs
As right this day as
Hundreds walk through,

A door opening and closing
On a passion closed
For good years ago.

Gene Lance

He misses the years after the war.
The tracts of houses springing up.
His first job the lead man gave him

a plumbstick and a sledge and said—
knock all the doorframes plumb,
but stay away from my house.

Hunched in a truck bed
he passed miles of half-built frames,
a single floor-plan flipped or flopped.

Wood so green the yardman said
he saw a 2x4 take root.
Joists spat into their faces as they

flew their commons in. High on
the roof ridge, as shadows stretched
past noon, they'd hail—singing

down at laborers on the ground:
Bring us more lumber! More nails!
We are the kings of carpentry!

Before Groundbreak

Off work and going upslope for a look
I left the plans, to see the view
their money bought, weighted with a rock,

and trampled a path of parted weeds
past pampas, nettles,
poison oak bristling in the breeze,

a weathered 2x4 nailed high up in a cedar's fork,
a haggard pair of panties waving
stiffly from a thorn,

I walked where they would walk.
Standing there, out of breath, where
they would stand, vacuuming,

or reaching for a towel, how bare
and graspable it will seem, and, ever-present,
our time and effort spent.

five

The World of Things

Setting Up

Dawn, and a wind blowing.
The hollow scrape of tools
Dragged out of a truckbed.

A Skilsaw leaned against
A stud. The collapsing sound
Of knitted cords dropped

On the subfloor. Smell of
Thermos and cigarette.
Morning's first agonized cut,

The blade shudders
And stalls. A shaft of sun
Slices down, flooding the block.

The World of Things

Bone-tired I nearly quit the first days.
Sixteen-penny brite box nails
bent on every blow and Dee said,

"We've done so many things,
you can't do anything well."
Mornings, Marvin wordlessly drove me

to the job, but once, offered—
"Don't let the wood push you around."
What words as homely could be as true?

It was easy to love carpentry then.
There was never rush or panic in Dee—that
now too familiar response to a world of things.

Soon I began to adopt the physical swagger
universal to men who work with their bodies:
an acceptance of weariness, of gravity,

of weight—and a defiant nonchalance
in response to it, the posture
recognizable in the hips and shoulders.

Jobsite Wind

that rips paper from the walls and changes plywood into sails
staggering a bent laborer with his load—
that curves string lines, bounces grass and trees in gusts

and makes the stick-framed studs above the ledger hum.
It searches us moving or standing still,
holding hammer or nailgun, our faces tight with cold

and hair wild. It searches us leaning into the day
for nothing we have, buffets the unprotected
figure atop the wall and one stooped above a half-framed floor

forcing blocks between the joists. Wakened
by the wind I drove deserted, limb-wrecked streets to the job
and found the roofless walls awash in wind, thrashing like a ship

in webs of lumber and shadows waving
above raindark floors laid purposeful with wood and nails.
Wind that threaded the trembling sticks of the house

driving plastic buckets down stairs, testing the corners
of a plywood stack, smearing a dropcloth to a wall like a shroud—
that rolled out of the throat of the world huge and articulate blasts—

And shoring spreadlegged, watching my hand hammering
in rhythm to my breath, the world hidden
beyond the nailhead's own demands

while inside a focused stillness intact and undisturbed
also incessant asked Who am I? Why this action?
What is this place I am in?

Nailer

Although it is a Sunday
across a cleared tract
of mud and standing water about the space of Disneyland
where dots of birds pick singly
and huge yellow *CAT*s and backhoes wait in Titan postures—
a carpenter, a pieceworker
is nailing on the solitary gray square of a new foundation,
flopping the plywood sheets down on the joists,
his hammer winking across the mud-brown expanse
and music from a parked pickup,
no walls yet, more like a dance floor than a house.

Bent down on his knees,
watching his hands work upon the plywood deck marked with
driven shining heads, he plays a game of thinking
separate thoughts, but drifts... the unbuttoned edges
of his workshirt swaying, right arm in a whipping motion,
left hand fat with nails.
By feel he turns the heads up, points down for the set and imagines
each brute particular fastened by a nail: one nail
for a puff of cloud, one for the shadowed hill,
one nail for the red tail on the ridge, one nail
for his pickup... one and one and one....
"six inches on center on the edges, twelve in the field"
—the floor honey like a field
but close-up, the grains run in exotic swirls
of rust and tan and chocolate brown, bits of cedar green, eddies
of blue, and gray when a sheet was used to cover a stack,

all between his knees, rippling, flaming
stitched in spots where the wood is weak, flowing
into pulses of black knots or flatter grains,
chunks of bark, mildew, delicate green scums... Sidling
on the floor, the denim of both knees worn completely through,
he daydreams on a sea of nailheads flashing
like wavetips...one and one and one and one....

But all around him are puddles the length of football fields
reflecting the sky in shapes
and gouged up through are the roots of trees,
balled-up wire fencing, buckets, fifty-gallon drums: debris,
and mounds bulldozed up
and ranged along the borders of the tract, embedded
with jagged chunks of concrete slab, galvanized
pipe bent oddly, stones the size of duffel bags
—here and there are smaller piles of concrete rubble heaped up—
    to be hauled away?
Or spread for fill?
A homeowner might find a buried layer beneath the soil in his yard.
Cement and sand and gravel, concrete
is what the world is built of, gushes rattling into
roads and dams, bears the iron of bridges in bay mud.
Green, it is as brittle as chalk
and warm to the touch. Two hundred years: it rots like wood.
In twenty-eight days the test cylinder of a seven-sack mix
is hard like real rock.

To the west, a monster storm pool reaches toward the road,
its surface silver, or steel,
the color of skyscrapers, steel. A man-high lumber stack leans
skirted in mud—the lowest studs completely sunk.
And the heavy equipment too is splattered over nicked and scratched

yellow paint—and their tracks and wheels and underpinnings,
the welded steel teeth and nuts as big as fists
are smeared and caked with clods and grass, their buckets
half-full of rainwater. Even the street ending
at the guardrail is brown, and at the intersection
a thousand muddy stripes shoot out.

I have worked on a similar, smaller job—
in the rain with two others, hauled a mud-slippery
concrete-shooting pumphose in hectic, sloppy efforts over
form walls, through boot-high water, first sliding, then falling,
trying to get the thing to budge, then, to get a grip,
the mix first clumping out like turds,
then arching into a stream, pushing the lead man back, his boots
slipping on the mud. The operator holds the four-inch squirting hose
to his genitals and calls it an "elephant's dick."
Two hundred feet long: six feet of it weigh a hundred pounds.

It is primordial, we serve it
banging on the forms to keep the concrete flowing, mud from it
on our hands, foreheads, noses, our clothes completely brown
even in our pockets—the driver
leaving the cab, walking to the hopper for a match as
rain showers on the pumper, the forms in the muddy field,
as the level in the forms rises
and the concrete begins to set.

Downslope

From a point across, the lot seemed floating down on seas
Of poison oak, hung on the hillside
As if on the back of a monstrous wave—
And spotting the long slope were shadows of scrub pine
In the heat and Sticky Monkey Bush
  And the lot was a bare field of plywood covers

Staked and sealed with mud, protecting the drilled holes.
Winched-down creaking
On the one-inch cable its grunting tonnage hung from,
The driller's CAT wore a groove in the road
And rutted the asphalt berm on the shoulder of the road
  Where the cable crossed to the *deadman*

That twisted and ovaled the hole it stood in
With the weight. Cuts two feet deep
Marked the slope where he spun a track, and the topsoil
And scree flung from the spinning drill
Was loose and drifted downhill in fanning alluvial flows
—The workmen lost pocket tools half-climbing,

Half-sliding down. The operator's helper, when the auger
Surfaced from a hole, signed him to stop
With a finger pointed to a tooth, then unwedged
The resinous roots from the cutting teeth. Across the slope,
The plain stripped twigs of it, coated with dust
  Still stayed nearly upright and oozed

The harmlessly poisonous, telltale black sap.
Mindless, the operator's helper yanked a bulbous
Blackened root as thick as a thumb
And pantomimed: thrusting and stirring its length
In a cunt in the air while the operator grinned.
  Then he bent to stroke a fingermark in the hydraulic grease

Flowing down the Kelly bar, as the auger disappeared
In the sandstone—the spirals
Of its turns, carved and smoking on the sides of the hole.
Standing beside them in the equipment's roar
Momentarily I felt afraid of falling in headfirst,
  Of struggling

Toward a spot of light above my feet,
When the operator inadvertently hooked a waist-high boulder
That burst from the ground clad in dirt, raw with the veins
Of roots, loose flakes; and he tried, wildly flipping
The yellow, loose-jointed controls to ease it onto
  The edge of the *CAT*'s blade while his man

Cursed, and shoved ineffectually, watching for his fingers
As the steel groaned, scoring a gray scar
On the wobbling stone. And then this memory: The stone,
As it casually rolled free—and the operator's helper,
Arms in the air, chasing it with feet pounding: running
  Madly down the grade.

Foundation

Slipping
clods, rolling
particles of
rock and mud:

what was shoveled
out down the
slope flowed
like lava over

their boot tops,
and filled each
tread that pressed
the sliding earth

to itself because
it was what
was solid and
bore their feet.

The Aftermath

And in spring poppies splayed from ash and seed
the city sprayed onto the fragile steeps.

Scorched foundations, concrete burnt
strangely pink, bereft even of mudsill—hosted

swimming poppies as did the hills
anywhere hose could stretch. Tradesmen

swam among them. Megaliths
of blackened chimneys, useless,

shedding new shadows; fence posts burned away
inside their concrete holes. Things sifting down

as the houses collapsed, fiery wall
to smoking floor to ground.

A mass of pennies, hidden like a nest
in the filth, its bowl and bureau gone.

A tray of silver, half articulate, half molten.
Sooted coins. A coat hook. A gutted house

demolished to build a house. House that
after seconds, the bulldozer rested

atop a pile of sticks, having crashed
through the dining room, and lifted the roof

off with its bucket. Then circling—with a tap,
folded each of the outer walls in. And tracking

the wreck to reduce its bulk, disturbed a nest
of bees that straggled out—lifted, and streamed

buzzing, furiously circling the abandoned
dozer, their sweetness stolen, lost, and

confused or alert to what had ruined them
—alighted—parading the yellow metal bulk,

wings spread upon air.

Oakland–Berkeley Hills Fire, 1991

Everything Under The Sun

From the station platform you can see them, the rooftops
over East 14th at sundown, mostly above
the depressed corner markets, the broke beauty salons:
    King's and Queen's
Hair Throne—the sun sparking flecks of light

on the lakes of tar and gravel littered with glass fifths
and pint empties. Below, the drag slides through the rest
of East Oakland or drifts into quiet, working neighborhoods lodged
between darker blocks, flattops beside flattops shading

the blistered gables of asphalt shingles, sagging and spotted
with coldpatch—the streets lined with pickups and campervans,
    mild yards
in golden crosslight, burnt brown, overgrown,
with neat chain-link fences, plaster statuary, bare dirt rose gardens

—the hard city soil a stratum of antstakes and engine oil
beaten to a powdery dust. Along a concrete drive
five Cambodian men dig out their sewer, joking, tossing
cigarettes in the trench, and up a block in the last light

two carpenters work tearing off a roof, their spades
shining a dim pink, dipping into the black widening hole.
An old woman watches them from her yard and remembers two
    carpenters before the war
swinging lunch pails with linked arms

walking to the trolley, as the carpenters above rip
through the thick, desiccated buildup of courses buckled and frayed,
coming off in striated chunks of tar and wood, each failed
relic layer, struck with twenty years of sun, shingled over till

new nails wouldn't grab in the black, disintegrating
layer the first roofer split and laid—*the lowest is always cedar:*
making a dust like grease that halos your sweating skin,
blackens kleenex at the sink—but the roofer's nose

was so used to the stink of cedar he said he couldn't smell it
and his scrawny back was reddish brown with the same sun
that fell on her old carpenters, and shone on her husband's greased,
     jet hair:
now he sits on the couch at the living room window,

washed in the light, contracted deep inside his disease; —and at a
touch
shingles crumble and fall through the attic, and the mass on the
     roof ridge
slides to the gutter, spilling near the barrow where a laborer stands.
She squeezes his arm; *His last stroke I told the driver*

to turn off his damn siren until we were out of the neighborhood.
Along the ridge the two men move slowly, crab-wise, flattening
the hundreds of small rusted nails that protrude, as bits of tarpaper fall,
looping toward the ground. At the roof edge: one of the two—

his shape, a black spot crawling across the sun.
From a back patio crowded with family a Mexican girl looks up
and stretches as she talks, feeling him look at her,
her bent wrists pressed to the small of her back, making chicken wings,

his attention drawing something out of her,
the way a boy's mouth drew blood through her skin and left the
    pink mark
she strokes absently, picturing herself
in the carpenter's eyes as he sends a dribble of roof dust

off the edge, a crown of sun above his head shining onto her skin,
    making her
feel weak, everything crisscrossing the world's face in giddy tides
as she hooks her toes on the bottom porch rail,
lying back, her little brothers skidding through the grass.

And across from them is a yard where a mason once stood, ball
    game on,
laboring on his own wall of brick with brick tracery and columns
    of brick,
talking with neighbors, the trowel clinking as he buttered one face
and one edge before laying a brick and trimming the mud,

each joint a sealed darkness beneath the crazed surface; the work
raising a course at a time on the quiet street—his patterns:
    herringbone,
fluted, and niched—each capital topped bizarrely with two bricks
leaning together, the upper, resting corners fast in a pinch of mortar.

Muse,

once present in a sapless tailing
of 2x4 as it fell from the saw;
in a hammerbent nail; in the
white unmuscled spine of a
weekend laborer; in winter sun.
Illusion?   Conviction?

       Crass confidence.

The Author

Mark Turpin is a carpenter. His poems have appeared in *The Paris Review, The Threepenny Review, Slate,* and *Ploughshares,* among other journals. In 1997 he received a prestigious Whiting award for a book in the Graywolf Press New Poets series, *Take Three: Two.* He is the son of a Presbyterian minister, and has two children. In 1999 he received the degree of Master of Arts from Boston University; otherwise, he has spent twenty-five years working construction and building houses as a crew foreman and master carpenter. He lives and works in the San Francisco Bay Area.